Io's Song

Io's Song

Signatures' Colors

(A Biographical Essay)

Murat Nemet-Nejat

chax

2019

ISBN 978-1-946104-19-9
Library of Congress Control Number:2019943807

Chax Press
1517 N Wilmot Rd no. 264
Tucson Arizona 85712-4410

Chax Press books are supported in part by individual donors, by sales of the books, and, from 2015-2019, by a fund at the University of Houston-Victoria. Please visit *https://chax.org/membership-support/* if you would like to contribute to our mission to make an impact on the literature and culture of our time.

Chax Press intern Katie Ray provided essential assistance, in design, layout, proofreading, and on other aspects of this book.

Cover image of Io (a moon of Jupiter) from NASA / Jet Propulsion Laboratory / University of Arizona.

Author Acknowledgments:

I would like to thank *160 Kilometre* for permitting me to include poems and fragments frommy translations from Sami Baydar's poetry and two poems from Seyhan Erözçelik's posthumous book *Kitap, Bitti(The Book, Finished)* in my book.

I would like to thank Runa Bandy Bandyopadhyay for permitting me to include a line from her book *Nocturnal Whistle* in my poem.

I would like to thank Michaael Hamburger's estate for including a section of his translation of Friedrich Hölderlin's "The Neckar" in my poem."

I would like to thank Haydar Ergülen for letting me use an adaptation of his poem "Pomegranate" in my poem.

"Language is the safe deposit of our souls that survives the checker in."

Night, behold, "the piano is playing scarletissimo." *(souljam)*

"Birds are like thoughts that the sky had after it had made its decision." (Kenneth Koch)

Dedicated to the Spirit of my Dear and Loving Friend Benjamin Hollander

Io's song

(a biographical essay)

I.

The secrets of a language're hidden, in another language.

oh, tantra

       tantra

the secret of my heart!

"In your own bud buriest, thy content.[1]" (W.S. "Sonnet 1")

"Fierce goddesses embodied in mystic syllables... visualizations of power
  centered in the [broken] body..." (Christopher Hareesh Wallis)

of words words words
             their ero-
                 tic

liquid

motherlodes emitting radioactive gold mines I can't stop them.

---

[1]   The Indo-European root of the word "content" is "tenere" (extension, desire), which in Hindu becomes "tantra" (vibration, weaving, music). In "*con*tent" (one side of the pun in Shakespeare's line, the other being "con*tent*")–a shift of accent–that desire , a.k.a. motion, is restricted.

motherfuckers

mag ma

       ablution

my grandma, entering the glory hole, and before taking a leak seven cups, after five cups,
empties on it. as if the centerfold of an underound
magazine.

An/kara: My Kind Hearted Step Mother[2]

Ankara.
An–: moment, second.
kara: black.
Ankara:
Second black, not first.
An(a): mother.
kar: doing it.
kar: snow.
kar(a): to the snow.
kara: land.
kara: black.
K(i)r: prick.
kar(i): the snow.
kari: old crone.
Kirhane: prick house
next to our synagogue in Istanbul there was a prick house,
on wooden tables at the end of Yom Kippur
in the dark, in the intersection of our street and theirs,
the ladies of the night and their pimps left
glasses of water for us to drink
for free: Sebil.
Mysterious Cybil.
So civil-
Ized.
Realized.
thirty years later I went to the same spot.
the synagogue and its porch garden
(where I'd spent two evenings a year, the twinkling lights mixing with the stars through the Succah)
was all in ruins,
the rusting gate ajar,
and a red rooster was strolling at home among the lunar mounds and weeds.
Red rooster: as in red light district?
Red: kizil.
(Kiz): virgin.

---

2   Ankara: my Kind Hearted Step Mother: the title of the poem is a line from the Turkish poet
Cemal Süreya. The bureaucratic capital of modern Turkey, Ankara is a step-mother compared to Istanbul,
which historically has been the beautiful, erotic tantric Turkish city. Another expression along these lines
is: Ankara is a wife, Istanbul is a mistress.

(Kiz): angry.
Yuzde yuz kiz: hundred percent virgin.
Yuz: hundred.
Yuz: face.
Yuz: swim.
Rooster: horoz.
Whore
and oz, as in the Wizard of O's.

II.

Cyclops

Freedom from perspective falling through receding walls of flat planes.[3]

_____

3   Noises proceeding from the heart of volcanoes were attributed to Cyclopses also. Due to his brain tumor, Benjamin Hollander lost all sense of depth during the last weeks of his life.

Prophecy & Space

face to face against a flat screen

eyes looking at each other through wires of amorous embrace,

apricots hanging from branches[4]

lines, parading against a flat sky,

strewn in the ever fluidity of montage

in the river of my eyes broken time passing

oh, weeping fragments of language

the flower follower of my soul

in the force fields of the wounded slashed */*

the *heightened graphicness of a life*

is revealed.[5]

---

4   While Nazim Hikmet and his beloved sitting face to face are looking into each others' eyes, apricot trees are in the background.

5   In *The Arcades Project*, Walter Benjamin asserts the dialectic method makes the experience of the past into an eternally fluid image by fracking into it and releasing its potency into the force field of a continuum... *in broken fragments of language*, what he calls "the broken temporality of montage." The dissolution of time, past and future, into a continuous present transforms depth in space into discontinuous, explosive slabs of consciousness—present-ness *revealed*: the prophetic dialectic image

Therefore, the stillness of collage in painting (or "avant-garde" poetry) becomes the dynamism of montage in film.

Gossip's Notations
                In a mysterious land
                words are drinking rum
                against the cold.
                return the gesture. (Sami Baydar)

Sweet lady, go sleep.

Space gossips,
                        touched, by the envious eye of the reader

nano interiors, unreal, parallel seconds reel in

space is a screen with a pin hole, dispersing the eye into words

contrapuntal solipsisms of erotic unions
the heart the hurt in the mirror

disperse
as if
one single sparrow's leaving its tail flying
                                from
the lagoon
of

traces

                        obliv
                                ion

Strike a match, your voice flamed in blue,
through the bright trees, your voice, the sounds of your tongue

Gossip's musical, its notes cracking broken words in aether—the eye pursuing lost Cybles, envied invoked Cain-like in the mirror.

are seismic blinks
in the innocence of *imp, limpid* image.

Sex Toy

A
q
u
a
r
r
e
l
In
the
k
i
t
c
h
e
n
Can
be
a
s
c
r
e
w
into
the
u
n
i
v
e
r
s
e

theatre

s/he is s/herlock holmes. dr. watson

pulls down his *calvin kleins*. violence, at bottom,

is a crack of yearning

she fell into the trap door of his love for her.

ardor's radar odor, a
door.

ariel ariel

she didn't fetch her hair along,
kept it on the dresser, full of despair,

but her hair fell through the unlit cracks,

I undid her drawers
I drowned myself in her hair.

Dashes

in the counter space

broken dishes

slash

this sadness above me, when will it stop brooding?

Io's Lament

calf sounds
half sounds
hoof signs
In the agon between the ear and the eye, sings drifts to signs.
eyelands
Grazing of Io in the Field

Gazing—a letting go, letting be, a magnetic junk food binge, consuming my interior
space.

signatures

the anorexic melancholy of loneliness

       the gray dawn

the lapin gloves of my awkward caressses
must be returned.

the moon resurects
the minarets.

death flies with a somewhat beauty

love, of
a not yet sensible Asia,
is the barely sensible skin of plants

in a democracy of the senses

water!

water!

Narcissus
Narcissus
   on the shore
    white petalled
seeps in,
narcotics
    looking absent minded

boiling water spoils

amor doloroso

it boils, a cloud of the sick.

the heat rises, this fire is this spring.

roots park up the tree, home

sick

under a cloud

no one home

when my wife cried
my servants told her to keep quiet
as i, while they kiss her hand,
see it in the mirror.

they embraced my wife, daughter,
making them drink herbs, i saw it in the mirror,
she sleeping, they worship her
by her bed.

together,
when i turn my back, I don't see what they are doing.

before my wife my servant
puts his forehead to the ground, from his back
the top of a creature is emerging
who listens to my wife like a child.

that's what they say, i know my wife
is pleading with me on the floor, but i see
her climbing someone in the mirror
sadly I love her.

my love lifts the weights from her body
and she, growing light,
can approach me
as the servant sees the blood on the floor
i see her crying in the mirror.

the servant is climbing down the stairs in the mirror
i see a postman arriving
the servant says there is no one home.

the clock chimes: hmmm

immense pool   **o**

              o

of sadness   o

           o

in an inner   o

         o

waveless   o   deep   *bird/toad*

      o

      because soundless

                       te

      because airless   i

                  d

O!   o

                 r

               h

             p

sundial's sandalled soundblast   **A**

"Is this the face that sent a thousand ships...?" (Christopher Marlow, *Faust*[6])

"you're" "no" "inspirer" "of" "beauty", "only" "a" "sea" " "whence" "inspiration" "comes"

"like" "shell" "born" "Venus" "with" "long" "disshevelled" "hair"

"or" "amphibians" "crawling" "on" "the" "shore".

---

6   The face belongs to Helen of Troy. To see and possess her is one of the wishes Faust wants the devil to grant him to purchase his soul. This is the first appearance of Helen (in a theatrical trick, out of a cloud) before Faust's eyes.

everything begins with the uttered sound sprung
from the pool
to aether

as if one single sparrow   'd left its tail flying.

disappearance

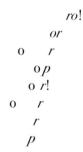

The Mirror

The pimp dropping encouraging hints on the other side of the doorway

on the other side,

the terminals're full of men and women and children,
accustomed to letting only their mouths be kissed
instead of doing their businesses kneeling down

lie d

off- key organ grinders, streetwalkers of music
abstractions from the harbor
infusing a sweet totality of death,
then drowning

this *lie d* blankets the ocean—no sea waves protruding.

quay

III.

at silences's threshold.

      The Garden Hears

A gardener hears this conversation
("*what about the one who makes it heard?*")
a flower was asking the garden one night.
("*I am condemned to this because of you,
and why were you?*")
and the garden pointing to the house, it smiled
("*may be someone may need to take a flower
to the cemetery?*")
since then, as if closing the lid of a coffin,
I lock the door of the house.

    .

in this new place, i'm dropping one letter from my name: oleander

I hear

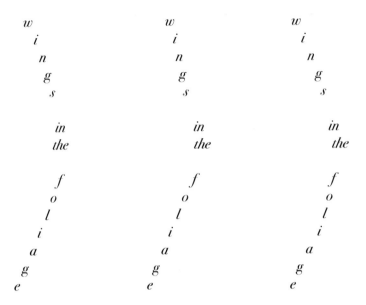

behind the wall

the eye sees the contradictions in words and sees through itself, in an act of freedom.

s m i t h e r e e n s!

To B. Hollander: an Elegy in the Shape Of an E-mail

*Dear Ben, finally, I wrote a godless version of Herbert's "Easter Wings" where the soul's
motions are pried loose from belief
by the senses.*

               Nymphs

words bathe in water

and explode

               on the other side

a new being is born

                    called flowering

a jonquil

river

          in the atlas fields

of dreams

where words as nymphs

                         cajole

apertures, slits

zeus

captured

Bee Sting

in the garden bees are nature, at the picnic table they're pests, in the mind they're divine. the Bee Sting explains everything. the sting becomes the *bee-sucking-the-nectar-shmearing-the-pollen,* a light current where nymphs play.

the year leaps, vows of silence. the black hole's suction pump fell quiet, before pouring.

as the gray dawn asks, "what's goin' on?"

In this new place I've dropped one letter from my name: oleander.

can see now that the ornate gate in the left, before which the floats are passing,
is the gate to an estate,
a scattering of willows behind its wall
there's half of a sumptuous villa on the right.

there are four spots of pure white in these pictures,
the iron gate on the left, a handkerchief hanging from the bridle of one of the horses,
the apron of the man walking behind the carriage
and the stucco walls of the villa behind the wall on the right.

IV.

A Needle Is Dropped On the Water

a potent liquid is flowing from my eyes

Raptors E-rupting

oh!
rapture's
rupture

supreme remembering

of the present

        isolate
               consciousness, an island

     in a sea *o*
     f forgetting

     oh, in a sea *o*
     f forgetting

the *great white* crosses and joins the captain's log book, dormant for a while — ripples.

but *noticing its own sound* in waves the sea gull panics, tilts one wing in

scans the irradiation of the puckered fire

42

Colors colors of death are everything, something one can hold on to survive, she said,
in the jettison flotsam of forgetfulness

On a skin
of sea crumbs

my mind
sores

On a skin
white as cream

by cock's
havoc
violated
in a hammock

Dream
and mid scream
and mid stream

She did once ask her lover, was their love now above fever?
I'm the horse by a river, it yelled, blind against its bit.

Venezuela - The Descent of Zeus

oh, zeus!
you deserted me
and i'm all blue.

blue plus blue still blue

Venezuela!
(can, I, dream) a conundrum of advent-
ures

        into space
        into the e ye   flesh light with a flashlight flush light ephemeral
into the ai r

   spilling   star   bat wing   dra wings

      s   vampire   i
                                 n

      p   ze us
                             s
      I   triangle   p   mirro
                  flying   a   bat
      n   tawny down drunk   c   b
                             e
      n   *Callgula*   Venus e Ella!
                           s
      I   d   I   h
                           o o
      n   r   n'm   t

      g   i   (K)   by a camera

      w   n   I   p
                             i t (y) less
      o   k   n   c   o
                             a s
      r   i   g   s

      d   n

      s   g

into d e s i r e

Annunciation

A si-
louh-
ette
(so-
h-
ul
peace)
is a
silly
hat.

at night
all the aches in my body lay geese
                                    in formation
flying

am am, an ice vermin, so human goose the ice block on which i crawl
is

spinitual words spunning in bodiless light
lightly, wishfully whistfully? whispfully -
whimfully, - whipfully whamfully -? wherefully
wombfully whichfully whorlfully, etc.

V.

> kin < kind

Dick-
in-
son

in jail

Dying In A Turkish Bath

did you ever attend a public bath?
I did.
the candle near me blew out,
and I became blind.
the blue of the dome disappeared.

they relit a candle on the navel stone.
the marble was wiped clean.
I saw some of my face in it.
it was bad, something awful,
and I became blind.
I didn't expect quite this from my face.

did you ever sob
while covered in soap?

Pornography

...................., flowing
peaceful along the sandy banks, whose water
halted her flight, and she implored her sisters
to change her form, and so, when Pan had caught her
and thought he held a nymph, it was only reeds
that yielded in her arms, and while he
                                        sighed
the soft air stirring in the reeds made also
the echo of a sign!

Rainbow

Rainbow is the first gauntlet of boast by God in the Bible. Serial criminals, hearing voices, emblazon their message in red on the mirror, rouge, blood, after having butchered their victim on the bed. The killer, drained, in its murderous ecstasy, does it say, remorseful, for that very moment, "I'm sorry. Pardon me. I'll never do this again?" Then, write the message in the surrounding space.

Hermes in Action, as an Agent for Zeus, Rescuing Io: the Play Within the Play[7]

Hermes bored Argus with stories
until all his eyes fell asleep

the story of Pan and Syrinx

was not boring but
opiate and herm-
aphrodite

warm and full of spume and dream
warm and scum
and her-
pes

a) Syrinx was a woodland nymph with many suitors
b) Pan (of the REED) chased her
c) Syrinx PLEADED with her sisters to change her into reeds
d) soft air moving through reed
e) as bleating through hoofs
f) sounding like a sigh
  Aye O   scything in the wind
e) Pan liked the sound
and bound them together with wax
and called them Syrinx
f) Hermes cut off his head
g) Hera put Argus' eyes on peacock feathers

---

7 The story of Pan and Syrinx in which Zeus through Hermes rescues Io echoes the main action of the myth where Zeus pursues and attacks Io.

Joy

For a period of fifteen years a recurring dream being inside a bath with a large pool,
smooth green wall tiles—a replica of a place I had visited with my family as a kid in the ancient
Ottoman city of Bursa—was! was! the only dream of unadulterated joy I ever had. The color of
the joy was green and its shape circular. I only remember entering that bath & waking up with
that feeling of joy. Nothing in between.

pour
n   *unicorn*

u-
cop-
ia

climbing a well
i saw stars

A cross.
An x.
A no.
A body.
A white.
A screen.
A perpetual.

Virginal

To bathe in your water
between your face and your hair
a hand must be.

Waters were alive, madly to love, links and links
I couldn't tell was it rose, was it house

I couldn't make it heard, your loving kiss
                              -es were like a mask, glued to my face,

to pull them out in memories,

        h   a   i   r   of torture

Hermes Bored Argus With a Story and Argus of the Hundred Eyes Listened

Subversion of what is Seen in the viSible

h airy

like Spanish moss on Louisiana oak

against the sky
like S- ask!- ia com-   d - o - n - t e - v - e - r !
        bing her hair sideways

spinning a thread of d- ove erotic words
in hOt bath tub   d a - m a s k

Varnish evanescing pink
full of swe at beads   d a h m - a s k   burying
sweet bear ds   d u m b !   into -
swan and swarm birds   Muriel's
                                                                                              burial -
horse and hazy   lazy ho urs   seen
                        wall
(in cerulean blue tile   s oh seductive hot bath house)
soul
am   c l o u d o f m i s t i n n !
(solemn!) as   but not solo Jack !

suc(cuba) cross(ing) in-
cubus
(ck)
cumb
c-
cul-
ent
mist

        cuba
                hairless in Cuba! h a i r l e s s h e r l a y e r s l a y s h e r l a y e r s i n c u b a !

suc   c   ulent mist

         s
         u
         b   sea
    cumb   blind -
         n   de-
         i   li...!
                                la(c
         g   h)!
         n   ah!
         i   pass-
         s   i've
         s   cissors   seed   s e a h m a n !
         o   or-
         r   dure
         c

haiti ebony
oh, comb!
O c c a m ‘s   s h aving charm

r a z o r !

Shearing the cloud   the cloud now is clear.
my blood spills on the ground, the cloud is modest,

blushes
and disappears.

your face shadows
in my palm
I see't and squeeze it,

drinking stars
from the urinal.

His face is almost gone
My desolation is pure,
The water is flat
My pain is on.

The bird crawling on your back and belly
and finally becoming a squirrel

Toes,
Toes,
Toes,
Toe nails,

Oh, my darling!

The sea visible, moon
us—a new kind of distance,
water exhilaration

substantial—as fields,
approaching me in the
black wings of

night, lay down, my pillow
split—my guitar
dew dropped.

My heart streaked
with moonlight blood—*indeed*! oh, in deed!
in dread

wings, let's

Swans
"Spinning within the span of a swan"

Swan milk in the bosom of the lake
withdrawn into the depth of the sky
flowing on earth
its history is upended
like Narcissus,

swan short of hands and legs
sensitive to water
its crimson eyes water's song
the lake doesn't fill, fast, let's cry, let's cry
swan
swan

the souls weeping in purple smoke
and being severed with silver wires maybe
are swan's blood
that spill out through willow's reeds

In the reflection of the peacock to
the ersatz stone reality abundantly defined
and stupidly too colorful, swan
is the weight

Out of the world of images it looks with vacant eyes
like a coaxed hand but with gloves
unaware like stars, drip by drip it rises to the sky

swan is water's joke
with gods
god's
with the living
swannesses
in a row
cover themselves in foam to shelter better in solitude in other warmths
from the reflective power of ruptures woven by your voice,

swan flying off
to the mouth of a stove where bread loaves are flying
kissing warmth sweats
swans stain the stars
as blindness descends over night

on the engraved graveyard branches of separation swan accumulates,
moves forward its talon
its eyes ceases dreaming
its lips withdrawn
stretches along each dimension of a square into our daydreaming,
if we keep quiet,
swan's blanketed its sleep with snow.

its eyes gather like wagons
then stretches the eye-lashes towards darkness
the interior world of
a glass-like waving cone sheared at the tip
the needles of a splash cutting their hands

swan singing comprehensible incomprehensible
in water's partitioned mouth kept ajar
swan is a severed neck amidst cries
there're herds of swans following behind in the wake of a corpse

even if the swan dies the lake can't pull back its lunar eyes
its chidren don't want, don't drink
its breast can't be milked
if a swan's born, the sky's received by the lake
swans deck stars round their necks
make make love, smelling smelling white grass

if you haven't seen a swan, just, just do so
their necks seem as if squeezed with light
where there should be departure, they meet

arriving just under my window   t
waking humanity from sleep
falling back, as if, it'll change everything.

Spinning within the span of a swan.   (Sami Baydar)

VI.

Juno gave the heifer (Io) to Argus (100 eyes) to guard
a. her condition was miserable
b. no one recognized her
c. spelled out her name on the ground with her hoof—
    white Heifer
        Io

- or + excess electron
is ionization

Zeus's
prank

sodden -

in a
cloud

rape hidden
in an Ionized cloud

TimeSpace Collapse

In Hera's defense/revenge of the young girl
Zeus ended with threads - filaments - of fleece in his hand
                    (*fils*
                    aimant)

See d

Seen is an escape
from *see d*
to be seen is to be a seed
eye is a procreation
to be *see d* is to stir seed and be fucked
to be the subject
to the eye—is to be desired—
I am *see d* by you
eye is the tong of knowledge
knowledge is two lumps of sugar.

how, how in social intercourse hearing, "I'm glad to see you," can we say, "thanks, I'm glad
to be *see d* by you too."
"nice to *see d* you"

therefore, *see d* is veiled as seen.

Cupid

Your
love
is
an arrow

the po   *apple*
                    quiver   ing aspen
am   *heart*
is

my
wound

railings of Notre Dame de Sion[8]

pubescent
knee socks
in pigeon courted
school

yard
surrounded
by

corpulent condors

with patient
beaks

endless
talons

(roosting
on
rail-
ings)

an-
gui-
shing

oh innocent school
girl
dreaming

of
doilies

---

8   Notre Dame de Sion was an an all-girl high school in the center of Istanbul started by the
French Children of Charity nuns (Filles de la Charité) in Constantinople in 1846 and still running
today.

and sacristy

and being
fucked

through

wool.

Door

"The midnight clock chimed: hmmm."

Think that all doors're closed
plead as if something's stuck
in your throat.... I never chalked a moon on the blackboard
let your tears choke me up, nights.

You don't know it, couldn't, you'ere a kid
not scared of the dark, like cats
we played in unlit gardens
becoming sleepy you slept on the dark grass
leaves fell on your body

During such nights did you say I put
like a shawl fearful nights on my shoulders
with a sweet trembling we amble towards the house
after we sleep it's winter
after we sleep someone's picking lilies.

Is the door ringing like a sword broken against a shield?
do i wear an armor, like a kid who grows up, and young
bumping against him and felling him *(feeling him)* going to open the door,
is it tears, is it rain, is it bramble

Moon Has Three Colors

a) white: full moon
b) red: harvest moon   (Io ='violet')
c) black: waning moon

"Io's priestesses performed heifer dance"
a) pretended to be driven by mad gadflies
b) woodpecker men tap[ped on doors calling 'Io, Io'

          asked for rain
          Glow Worms

god flies of ecstasy

Another Biographical Sketch, Boyhood Dreams

It was a grimy scene, the stuff of which high school dreams are made of. How do you make love in the back seat of a car? After all cars are narrow, inconvenient places. But the thrill of it! In the dark. The resistance of the girl. Importuning. Momentary, ardent promises. Repositioning of the girl's legs to create more space, perhaps hooking them over his back. The teen-age kid, pants to the knees, kneeling on the floor...

But this time the young man is in his thirties. The spot is not a lover's lane but the corner of an empty city parking lot. In the November moonlight one can see small collections of garbage along the wall. The girl is not Sandy sitting three rows ahead in his class, but a black New York City hooker. Her panties are not half down her knees in a process of seduction, but taken off for convenience sake. No anxiety, overwhelmed by superior will, in her eyes, but patience.

But on the man's part what ardor, what passion. He's on his knees. His trousers and underwear in one joint action pulled down but not removed. He's actually groaning. "Oh, baby what sweet legs you have. Oh, sweet baby, you're wonderful, beautiful." Snuggling his nose into her dark pubic hair. Squeezing her thighs, sniffing, deeply inhaling, "Oh, baby how sweet and wonderful you are," giving her thighs little lover's bites...

In effect she is quite beautiful, long legged, with a red silky dress.

The woman shows her first expression in her face. Shock? Surprise? A big, black man appears at the window. Another behind him watches. Yes, in shock at seeing him, she tightens her legs against the face of the man working between her legs. The man takes this to be a response on her part to his capable tongue, and he feels good. He scrambles to penetrate in a joint climax.

Then, the man opens the door and hits the john on the head, only twice. The man crumples in mid action. A narrow line of blood trickles next to his ear. The woman, in genuine annoyance, says, "Oh, man, did you have to waste him?"

"Get out the car, bitch, and get lost."

The two man perform on him all the rituals that will be performed on white men murdered in a parking lot in Harlem in midnight.

VII.

Afraid of Jove, and worried over his cheating,
She (Juno) turned her (Io) over to the keeping of Argus
Who had a hundred eyes... No matter how he stood,
Which way he turned, he always looked at Io,
Always had Io in sight...

........; two at a time,
No more than two, would ever close in slumber

Rainbow

I is
me,
see!

the sea,

the eye
in the sky,

the d- -me castigated globe
     o o-   eyeglasses   of the heart.
of the   orb

The Nile
"The barge she sat in, like a burnished throne,
Burned on the water...." (*Anthony and Cleopatra*)

Purple the sails, and so perfumèd that
The winds were lovesick with them. The oars were silver,
Which to the tune of flutes kept stroke, and made
The water which they beat to follow faster,
As amorous of their strokes.

On the arms of the maternal smell
barbarians' scars.

Hermaphrodic pronouns.

He made love biting her own lips.

Her delights d o l p h i n - l i k e

they showed her penis above the ailments
he lived in

Clitoris arose dahlia!

ah, my c-l-i-t-o -p-e-t-r-a

a rose!

bitten tenderly

                    The barge she sweated in...

I sat on his sweet bud.

Stood pretty dimpled boys, like smiling Cupids,
With divers-colored fans, whose wind did seem
To glow the delicate cheeks which they did cool,

... what they undid did.

Visual Effects

        (Io) became
What once she was, again; the bristles vanish,
The horns are gone, the great round eyes grow smaller,
The gaping jaws are narrower, the shoulders
Return, she has hands again, and toes and fingers,
The only sign of the heifer is the

                   whiteness.
              Of Id

She stands erect, a nymph again

(*yet*
                still fearful
That speech may still be mooing...)

Now people, robed in linen, pay her homage,
A very goddess, and a son is born,
.........., the seed of Jove

the afterlife
of Io

(an autobiography)

signatures' colors

" .... And O you
Lovely Ionian isles where the sea breeze

Wafts coolness on hot shores and runs rustling through
And oh, where still a golden autumn
Turns into songs the poor people's sighing,

Where their pomegranate ripens, the orange glints
In a green night and richly the resin drips
From mastic trees and drum and cymbal
Beats to the wild labyrinthine dances.

To you, perhaps, you islands, my guardian God
One day will take me; yet even then I should
Recall my Neckar, loyal to his
Amiable meadows and bankside willows."
("The Neckar,[9]" F. Hölderlin, translated by Michael Hamburger)

---

9   "The Neckar" is the river near which Friedrich Hölderlin grew up in Germany. The poem
starts with a pre-Wordsworthian effusion of love for the Neckar as a place of motherly love and
tenderness. Then, suddenly the poem jumps to a different, wilder kind of home which Hölderlin longs
for and his heart belongs to. The passage quoted above starts exactly at that startling transformative
moment in the poem and continues to
the end.

VIII

The Open Garden: Tangential

w' experience light as capturing something, but light's only going through's

hear,
here!

Falling by the Bird's Light

somewhere else, z

m!

*there
's there!*

"... Rivers, 'ivers
why're they the Almighty's joy?
             but, but how could 'e, otherwise
Descend?
...
... With deep bedded reason they run,
through dry land. but all that 'e **hears**
's

a sign."[10]

  *"cutting a slice of watermelon to woo you.
             i split my heart."*

10   A fragment from F. Hölderlin's poem "The Ister." The Ister is the ancient Greek/Thracian
name for the Danube, which starts in Germany and drains southeast into The Black Sea.

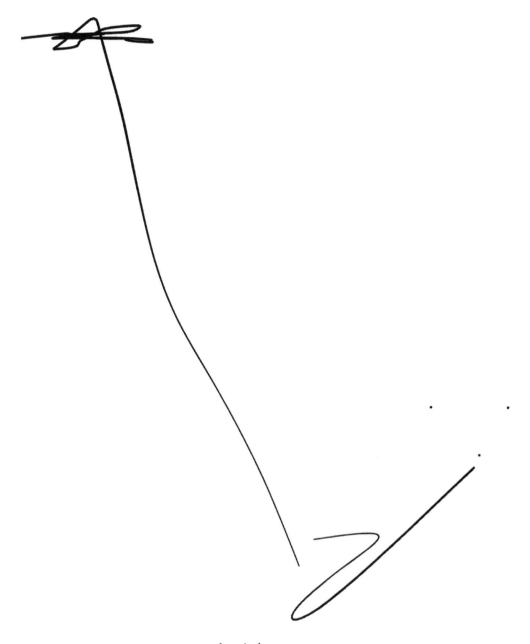

the wind
dark

sea

arrived at.

cyclops's
one-eyed home.

the enclosed park

"words, words, words
names!"
   (*camels and weasels*)

in the arms of the eternal--Odysseus

departure
in the concave mirror
arrival   return

in the mirror
departure
in the mirror
arrival

in the mirror
arrival

in the mirror
departure

river
is
a mirror

is[11]

---

[11]   Cyclop's one-eyed vision compresses, arrives at tautolgy.

my soul blankets the ocean, no see waves protruding.

wind
wind

sea

the renaissance invents perspective

fights
windmills

doesn't see

the
wind

IX.

Para/Dice
Parade/Ice[12]

Hercules's Pillars
"The heart yearns for departures. In the v a g a b o u n d a r y of the sea." Ulysses
"But the subject of all myths's arrival." W. Benjamin

---

12   The Greek root of Parádeisos is an enclosed park. But the whole history of paradise in the west is about expulsion.

Cause and Effect, a Linguistic Play: the Metaphysics of a Poem
"We think words are for us, we're for them."

While

   in our daily life cause precedes effect ("Nothing comes of nothing"), i.e., cause is the cause of effect–they're the same. In language a new meaning is its own cause (*because of effect*), effect *imagines* cause, it is the original cause of effect. In the mirror of language one experiences the world upside down, time is reversed (or, paralyzed, time frees itself and dissolves into air…). We see the future as the past. Etymologically, each word has infinite openings lying **be**-fore it. But once a direction is taken, just at that moment language materializes a new meaning for that sound and instantly another infinity opens around the word (as if expanding waves around a pebble, or Basho's frog, casting itself into the water). Time in language's built by a series of instantaneous transformations that while we imagine that the old meaning is the builder of this home, its original cause, a brick. Whereas what we have is endless expansion, tracing the motions of endless soul. Whereas the cause is just a whim, a stirring of the wind, occurring that instant, *Not Necessary*. Absolutely necessary in the ocean of the imagination, of which words are just waves, meaning is just what we can see, looking into the darkness of ourselves, into its infinite dangers and riches in which we are a momentary dream, surrounded by dreams. What we call universe, what we call language.

   A selfie depicting oblivion surrounds the individual dream into which I wake…. I dream I'm wading.

enthropy of the stars

memory! o, memory!
thy name is forgetfulness!

advancing at the speed
of the soul
from recessive regions of
Elen
é!

shining shining shining shining
shining shining shining shining

farewell, dear Ben.

farewell, dear Ben.

A Flat Portrait of Departure

Art's delirious.
in that painting while it depicts the lengthening of a
swan
Angels are hiding in the spot where the lights
falls
and where demons the creator and liquid nymphs
are ruling our sight

The portrait resumes moving
(that carries You within itself)
To pass through some lights and shadows
it will create same thing each time

As for me, I will look at it remembering the original creator
Comparing you to an elongated swanlight will fall just from the front
onto your eyes.
For the sake of silence a pleading full of aches
That is like a naked baby in the garden of
snow.

My swan of snow elongated to reach light
Full of fields belonging to the portrait of departure
Utter a few things with words--say I love you
Angels are hiding in the light reaching you   (Sami Baydar)

X.

spirit is flesh,

hundred eyes collapsing into the black hole of dying,

then expands
a spring
into a horizon

event horizon [13]

on the Black Sea the horizon
bends, does not become
itself.

There's imperfection in the horizon. simply—

all the fishermen know this.

before them is death, childhood, families behind.

that's how it is.   {Seyhan Erözçelik)

---

[13]   The Turkish/German director Fatih Akın's film *The Edge of Heaven* ends at the same spot, on the Turkish shore of the Black Sea the son waiting for his father to return from fishing. Erözçelik himself was born and grew up in Bartın, a town on the Black Sea.

The Matter of Signals

I'm fish. Am out o' fish.
I bought yellow tulips. Tulips,
red. Yellow tulips
Shed their petals. Red
tulip's standing.

Then I kept saying
"we're forty,
know each other

The voice came
"forty urns
with broken ears...
for tea..."

Saying that, mild submission was done with
fight was done with
there's still no blanket.
and I don't need candles
when you snuff them out
they smell!

I don't like c o n f a l   g r a t i o n s, that's how it is.   (Seyhan Erözçelik[14])

_____

14   "The Matter of Signals" and "event horizon" ("mist on the black sea") are from a
collection of twenty-four poems that Seyhan Erözçelik wrote in the final days of his life (died in 2011).
Posthumously published in 2018 by *160 Kilometre* under the title *The Book, Finished*.

"my leg... surrounded by melancholic water kiss." (Runa Bandyopadhyay)

a desert, of vibrations, attached to infinite pool

fata morgana.

a there that is anoth'r there, bent

light

the finite and infinite reconcile with'n a given set—
infinity of thirst like a viable dormant
egg lying within the fluid givens of each word.

heedless fragments of broken, amorous dreams,

absorbed by a single eye

in a clarity of montage

depth bursts into flat layers
of yearning

each yearning enters a mist

A Dialhectic Poem

A poem is experiencing a writer's block, unable to access the Muse.

brooks of heaven flow.
go chanting the divine name;
birds, alive, curve, draw
holy circles in a game.

gentle trees glow in gold,
their young roots disdain the earth,
their hungry roots searching upwards
wash down their thirst with allah's name.

older branches bend; ripe
with weight they understand,
gently observe the red rose pray
mad with perfumed flame.

new-born souls bite the tight-skinned fruit,
smiles shine on them in gold;
they sip the outpoured juice, taste life's end,
receive the clothes of Paradise.

their fair faces round as the moon,
their soft words fresh as the morn,
wise houri girls play among souls,
ponder with them on allah's name.[15]

---

15   This poem is an adaptation of a poem by the 13th century Turkish poet Yunus Emre.

XI.

"... Names are as the morning breeze
... fall, like error.
upon the heart..."[16]

---

16   A fragment from F. Holderlin's "Patmos."

Epitaph—Wind Through the Cypresses

o, mother of Eléné⁷ the victim of an unspeakeble ac
t,

victor o,
'er,
anguished

beauty

        Sing t'me of the man Moūsaī⁸ the man of twists and turns

        driven time'n again off course, once he h'd plundered, the hallowed
        heights of Troy.

argos w as a foreign country whose language Odysseus'd learnt.

---

17   Like the spinning of a Katoshka doll into itself, the same obsessive compulsive myth of violent sexual attack—and transformative eruption and suffering and beauty (a sign of moral perversion of the skies)—spins within itself: a bird and a maiden—Zeus and Io, Leda and the Swan, the Holy Ghost and Virgin Mary, Child and Parent.

18   Moūsai: the sound in Homer's word for "the muse," also the sound of Moses' name in Turkish (Musa). Mus(e)-vi: Jew.

The sky *droopsshimmer ing* into the *gravity* of water.

The infinitely small vocabulary of a diagonal so-so paradise.

      Fatal Crews of Odysseus

Eden spins tautologies. That's the mirage of depth, suppressing the reality of death
in another space. god is everywhere. How can He know depth. can't feel perspective.
Divine language is flat. Departure's arrival,

as one shuffles off this mortal coil (this coffin), the universe flattens. tosses vertical.

                    wind
                    wind
                    wind

                    wound
                    wound
                    wound
                      see

Argos

    Argos was Odysseus's dog that recognizes disguised Odysseus at his return home to Ithaca, by dropping its ears and wagging its tail. Too old and decrepid, then it dies. Odysseus passes by shedding a tear without dropping his disguise.

A Digression: Tieresias Responds Angrily to Oedipus's Bullying Query, in the face of silence, and Finally Answers His Question

O miserable Power
One-hundred-eyes'-all-seeing and blindness are one
You'll fall into the eternal flatness of dark
Know answer is my answer
Know thyself

What was your tragedy, you foolish man
that you fucked thy father and killed your ma
Or that you were enlightened by no ledge
you are at the edge of precipice
and doth not know it.

XII.

      the migration of ions

during the day, the color of the Aegean is turqoise.[19]

the Greeks called it the *I'onion* Sea—that part of Anatolia they'd colonized being called *I'onia*.

He wandered its islands in the great poem of wandering and exile, towards home, Ogygia, Aeolia, Circe, Phaeacia of Naussica, played by Rossana Podestà in the film by Mario Camerini, and the island with no name inhabited by the Cyplops.

Eipheson was the great city of *I'onia*. Homer never mentions it because *it* was written earlier.

the *Iliad* celebrates the original liberation of Io from the *barbarians-of-a-thousand-stars* Trojans, in response to Helen's theft by Paris.

we in the west celebrate this sacred virile event of carnage while having sex, in our condoms, receptacles for our seeds.

Trojan is also the talisman against the cuckold Menelaus[20] who started the whole messy saga of Agamemnon's murder by his wife Clytemnestra[21] at his return home (also himself cuckolded), taking a shower, and his being revenged by his son Orestes by the killing of his mother.

---

19   The poet Lale Müldür called turqoise the Turkish green in her book *the book of series*.
20   Menelaus was Helen's husband.
21   Clytemnestra also was from the seed of love between Zeus and Leda. Two brothers had married two sisters.

Reintegration

When my dad moved and later brought his family from Iran to Istanbul, he adopted a new signature in Latin characters. From an unlit corridor entering his study in our Istanbul apartment as a kid, I saw on his desk pages on which he h'd scribbled practicing a florid version of his public name "Seifollah" (*the Sword of Allah*) over and over again.

My parents were Marrano Jews, in Iran, pretending to be Moslems, while practising Judaism in secret. He'd a warrior Moslem name and a meek Jewish name, the stuttering Moses's brother Aaron's, able to speak clearly and glibly, the *Torah*'s first politician and bureaucrat, the starter of the line of Cohens, the Jew St. Peter.

enigma[22]

Seif -	s'word	Safe + - - - - -	Sx
O -	of	Sword	
llah	Allah	my dad	
		Aaron's	

I fell   (Bible's

over the   first

I fell   bureaucrat)'s   clear - off! cone head!

tower   +   -   speaker

$$-1 + 1 = 2$$

as Brut -   Marronic/Koranic

e   Gnomic/Byronic

over Caesar'   pussy

s negative s-   aggressive safe arctic

word   name   goon   Mose e aic   start ler

---

22   To Alan Turing the problem of his own sexuality within the English society of the time proved more intractable than the Nazi code.

stutter
birth's
gno -
m an -
cla -
ture

Chaff

          im   ding words
     sin   p l o p l o
     tax   ex   ding dong a trophy - alas! - entrophy
sunday   in Claus   trophobia
          S a n t a
          Pyhrric
          heart

                    wife

menelaus, the cuckold: A Narrative

leda   zeus
elene   aechilles   swans
aphrodite

return home

clytemnestra agamemnon ablution by death

antigone electrified orestes

A mistiness after the rain,   hammered with pain[23]

---

23   Electra and Antigone, two female figures who instigate action against the status quo instead of being suffering victims of acts by male gods or humans. Hölderlin translates *Antigone*, her embodiment of sacred rites for the dead.

Fracking: Meditation On a Text by W. Benjamin[24]

"... to reefer is to explode..."

                                  extracting

                                                magazine rocks, from the phantasmagoria

of biography,

                an infarctsis of the heart

liquidifying into a new image
                         of

sashaying dialectics

the pulverized love

                ache,
                      in the crisscross
                                    bull's eye

        of the lover and the loved

        a kiss

light striking from one end to the other

---

24   The text is from Benjamin's essay on Proust. While the essay explores Proust's exploration of "the recapturing of time," the piece also reveals the illusive nature (but potency) of what's revealed: memory as a rabbit's hole, a children's telephone game played with what one calls the past, and is framed as memory. Beginnings, and endings, are ionized clouds. In other words, memory is the space of imaginary numbers: the square root (the recapture, only in the heart) of a loss.

the compressed eyes, sharing the space of one bed
　sharing two-eyes, lovers
　in one bed

　　　　　　O Cyclops! O Benjamin, o Benjamin, where did you

　　　　　　disappear? Did you go to Hollan'?

"*Where were ye, Nymphs?*..." (J. Milton, *Lycidas*)

XII.

       Hölderlin hears voices thru the wall in his cell

they maroon the virulent Penis in a rubber room,
shuffling there the elusive floors endlessly,
kept straight
in a straight jacket:

seeeeeeeeeee ds o' my featherly father!

       fuck me
       fuck me

where your face ended and my body began,
that's to say your neck...

sitting on the face

the part of your body i can't remember's
the face.

object/ivity, of the subjective

talcum powder, squat vaseline jar,
a queen bed
always covered
with a bed spread,
humiliation
visible in the ceiling mirror.

there

my
silhou
ette

Multiplications Of Passion In This Cursed Triangle

is a drop of death
seen from another angle
seen from another angle
seen.

(sea
clop)

"... the calf's ended
tangled
in the tether

it broke..." (F. Hölderlin, "on pale leaf....")

brain cancer

cruising
the
wind wind
sea

Rocks'n Breaks of the Heart

Intensity of feeling is words' inability to arrive at their illusive destinations. Intensity's
that distance. Obstructions of rock on the path of the sentence—where words deep
in their failure—turn words into optical objects of desire, projecting the reader's interior
longings onto those rocks,
        oh the difference of knowing that what is merely visible is woven
        into what is longed for, and spelling out
        that what is merely accepted is in conflict with what is gossiped about
                                              trans-
forming them back into words. The rocks of pain in the heart are words. *Io's Song* are those
rocks, fragments speaking to each other *(like the motions of deceptive ghosts in photographs,
aroused by light's arrowing errors or charlaton's tricks. Oleant colors!)*. The I and the eye
truly join, and the eye, *shredded and restored*, becomes the window to the errant soul,
                    the object
                                -ive domain of the spirit. Did you see the soul
walking? The invisible talking? The reader enters this space, romps at his/ her peril.

      Wait, the time's ripe
      lambs have long been in their pens
      the baaing ceased
      the angels of the stable arrived.

      The one passing thru at night
      must be a merchant
      who can see the bees in the dark
      the straw chaff
      but must be a man who can melt
      all this in one go
      into one.

      The given paradigm is a bird
      rapt in its own reverie
      the collar of reverie around its neck.

      Why shouldn't the inside of my eyes
      be without yellow stars
      streaked with broken clouds
      i'll go like a pedigree horse

if you want me to get lost.

go like a pedigree horse
these are my shapes...

pouring from one river to the other

only pebbles of pain will be left to you.

s ill ts

syrinx

my soul is a jelly fish without a womb
light descend in the gutted out space of the dome.

XIII.

Degas's "Woman Drinking Absynth": Moments of Visual Articulation

Looking at Degas's "Woman Drinking Absynth," I'm startled by the her complete oblivion to her pose, lost someplace between that drink and her eroded life. The painting's pathos (its bottomless sorrow)'s there because Degas is painting a space, subjective shifting to objectivity (the man at the next table as articulated), not art, not an ego-contered concept of form... but the space of her ravished, soon almost to be made invisible soul.

"...
To you, perhaps, you islands, my guardian God
One day will take me..." ("The Neckar")

Pomagranate

Winter is too vast let's go to the pomegranate
the surface of the day grew cold, to the pomegranates

a thousand warm words strew the summer

my tongue dry, from here let's go to the pomegranates
pomegranate has a house, very crowded

I wish we lived there too
the house too big

every room a distance, children closed boxes
the back yard a chaos. When we split grapes

how we were vinyard friends, it seems,

she, garden to love, the insane bird a creeping ivory
holding my small hand to my love, now, let's go to the pomegranates
(Haydar Ergülen}

sadness fell on words prior to the skin
        the raven swooped o'er the orchard,
before the tongue felt cold felt sad.

Nietzche's Hatred
            for F. Hölderlin

Plato's
a tease

A sophist

His tongue on thought's g-spot

Nietzche knew this, perhaps why he hated him (also

a poet).

Also a poet

he chose to *diiii e*
going iiiin ward

kissing a dumb
suffering
horse
in Turin.

"M" Sees "A" In His Dream

A dinnah

Denied to me

I touch
The glass
Of the window

The moonlit night is cold cold

The table
beckons

Beckons
Alas...

Oh! dinna!

Wombles: A Lullaby
(first written at the request of my grandson Abey that I write a poem for him)
for my grandchildren Abey, Hannah, Benny, Lola, and Gen-Gen (Cleo)

I knew of a pig with a pink nose
It always hunted with its nose for truffles
But that was not enough
It entered our kitchen and ate my breakfast waffles.

And I knew of a Siamese cat with big whiskers
It always scooted in the room without a whisper
But I knew when it meowed
It was asking for my cucumber pickles.

And I knew of a dog with drooping ears
called Wombles, that when I took a bath
It chased after the bubbles
I laughed and laughed that took away all my troubles.

when quinces become pomegranates
you become mine,
when above our troubled heads
the world's translucent.

Peeping Tom

The woman
Passing the soap
Along the
Curves of her body,
One leg up;
The soap appears
And disappears.

What likes ice cream, sex and lives in a dark place? Tongue.

The Problem Poem: *Io's Song*, a Crisis of Reading

Io's Song—a combination of visual poems, poems that play around the sounds of words or poems that are based on word breaks or parallel fragments of phrases, etc. on the page, the total effect of which is an optical code. The common quality among such poems, where the darting eye plays a primary part, is twofold. First, they are basically unreadable—insipient poems emerging simultaneously on the page, clamoring for attention—by one single person forced to make a choice out of his or her inner being, not by the *given* dictates of syntax or other "objective" structure on the page. Something in their appearance, ambiguous and paralyzing, inexorably leads towards silence, a kind of muteness or askew sounds or movements of language. *Io's Song* is a human voice speaking in an aliem medium, through the mouth of a cow. That is the poetics dimension of the Io myth, the "Syrinx music" embedded in it.

The objective ambivalence on the page forces the eye, sparked discontinuously (and continuously) by the brain, to be the sole arbiter of deciding how to read or proceed reading. In other words, to a crisis of reading aloud.

The second problem is that all parts of the poem together, in a proper sense of what art or form should be or is, make no sense. In that respect they are feral, savage, totally raw. I gave a reading of parts of the first section of the poem at the Poetry Project in 1995. I was still into the spirit of the experience of the poem and could enter into the gaps some of the visual poems created moving, pulling in all sorts of directions. The result was an odd series of verbal animal sounds, totally improvised at the moment, totally open ended, totally at the mercy of the moment, by the end of which one of my poet friends told another "someone has to tell Murat that he had gone insane."

I never could experience or repeat the performance of that reading. The poem became unperfomable *as a sound*. Once out of the trance of writing it, it receded into silence, muteness for me, something that was, to me, a source of great disturbance. I could not enter however hard I tried into the spirit or the trance, making the improvisatory experience of the poem impossible (at its origin possible, the writing of which being the truly improvisatory, not previously existing performance). The poem became experiencable in silence through the eye; but un-performable—*or a performance involving silence*. That is what I call the crisis of reading. Ever since that day every poem I write became an avenue of exploration, a gateway into another black hole.

Further Notes: On Myths

a)

The eye always sees more than the tongue can speak. (That's what leads to a crisis of reading.) The eye enters the mysteries of the soul (of the world) more fully than words can. That's why also a true traslation (entering the mysterious totality of
another language) or a citation (entering the totality of human wisdom in language) must always be visual.

b)

Telephone Call In the Digital Age

Dial one if... lyric

Dial two if... epic

Dial three if... tragic

c)

Myths

Myth is not a narrative applied, but dis-covered. The narrative that emanates against our will revealing ITSELF, A VIOLENT LIGHT that descends and leaves. Every myth is an arrival and escape, departure which in truth is death. This is due to the nature of words, their will to metamorphoze themselves from meaning to meaning, AS
BEEING, crossing boundaries across human will, human reason or human culture, seeing ourselves thru the mirror of language as a reflection, willess, bobbing on the alien surface (façade) of words, ceding to insanity to plumb its depths.

d)

nightingale descending into the darkness of night, waiting

you'll ascend the stairs slowly
on your skirts a golden pile of leaves
always you'll be looking at the East crying

Always looking at the East crying to be revived

waters are yellowing ... your face paling in shadows
bending roses bleed bleeding to the ground
wait flame like on branches nightingale
has water burnt why is the marble bronze

From yellow to bronze to crimson to night is the fiery movement of the soul in its ascent.

Fire is reflected light in the evening twilight, soon to be replaced by the reflected light of the moon.

The nightingale and the branch on which it stands become one, waiting together.

wait flame like on branches nightingale

look at the crimson sky turning evening   (Ahmet Haşım)

e)
Get up, before your skull is dust ridden
fill up your glass before your grave is sodden

Since since the last motel is the valley of silence
scream to the sky now, before the night is in

Please my sylvan beauty, on your being
do not leave my dust be, before your shadow has been

let the sparkle of the glass tinder existence
the deed of your plot will not before your sin

Reader, don't forget Hafiz's words
take a bath in your tears, then on beauty sing! beauty's wing!   (Hafız)

f)
A gazelle jumps down drinking water among the reeds.   (İlhan Berk)

About the Author

The critic Maria Damon writes on Murat Nemet-Nejat's last book *Animals of Dawn*: A radiant matrix of intertextuality, *Animals of Dawn*, in holding a vast array of precedent texts –as disparate as *Hamlet*, "Un Coup de Dés," and Basho's famous frog haiku –in constellated suspension, creates an aubade-as-web-of-wonders in which we animals wake from our sleep to the marvels of language as the impossibly strong, invisibly powerful net that sustains us all –texts, sentient beings, texts as sentient beings and vice versa –in electric, vibrating relation.

Murat Nemet-Nejat is the editor and translator of *Eda: An Anthology of Contemporary Turkish Poetry* (Talisman 2004). Poet, translator, essayist, a number of his books include the poems *The Spiritual Life of Replicants* (Talisman, 2011), *Animals of Dawn* (Talisman, 2016), *Io's Song* (Chax, 2019); the translations Orhan Veli. *I, Orhan Veli* (Hanging Loose, 1989), Seyhan Erözçelik. *Rosestrikes and Coffee Grinds* (Talisman, 2010), Ece Ayhan. *A Blind Cat Black and Orthodoxies* (Sun and Moon Press, 1997; Green Integers, 2016), Birhan Keskin. *Yol* (Spuyten Duyvil, 2018); the essays "Questions of Accent" (*The Exquisite Corpse* 1993; *Thus Spake the Corpse: An Exquisite Corpse Reade 1988-1998*, Black Sparrow Press, 1999), "A Godless Sufism," (Talisman, 1995), *The Peripheral Space of Photography* (Green Integers, 2004), "Dear Charles, Letters from a Turk: *Mayan Letters*, Herman Melville and *Eda*" (*Letters for Olson*, edited by Benjamin Hollander, Spuyten Duyvi, 2016), "A Dialogue with Olga" (*Olga Chernysheva/ Vague Accent*, The Drawing Center, 2016).

Murat Nemet-Nejat is presently working on the poem *Camels & Weasels* and the translations of selections from the Turkish poets Sami Baydar and küçük Iskender's poetry. "

About Chax

Founded in 1984 in Tucson, Arizona, Chax has published more than 240 books in a variety of formats, including hand printed letterpress books and chapbooks, hybrid chapbooks, book arts editions, and trade paperback editions such as the book you are holding. From August 2014 until July 2018 Chax Press resided in Victoria, Texas, where it was located in the University of Houston-Victoria Center for the Arts. UHV has supported the publication of *Since I Moved In*, which has also received support from friends of the press. Chax is a nonprofit 501(c)(3) organization which depends on support from various government private funders, and, primarily, from individual donors and readers In July 2018 Chax Press returned to Tucson, Arizona, while maintaining an affiliation with the University of Houston-Victoria. Our current address is 1517 North Wilmot Road no. 264, Tucson, Arizona 85712-4410. You can email us at *chaxpress@gmail.com*.

Recent books include *A Mere Rica* by Linh Dinh, *Visible Instruments* by Michael Kelleher, *What's the Title?* by Serge Gavronsky, *Diesel Hand* by Nico Vassilakis, *At Night on The Sun* by Will Alexander, *The Hindrances of Householders* by Jennifer Barlett, *Who Do With Words* by Tracie Morris, *Mantis* by David Dowker, *Rechelesse Pratticque* by Karen Mac Cormack, *The Hero* by Hélène Sanguinetti (transl. by Ann Cefola), *Since I Moved In* by Trace Peterson, *For Instance* by Eli Goldblatt, *Towards a Menagerie* by David Miller, and *The Long White Cloud of Unknowing* by Lisa Samuels. You may find CHAX at *https://chax.org/*